AF228149

FOOD
MARKETING

BY KURT WALDENDORF

Essential Library
An Imprint of Abdo Publishing
abdobooks.com

ABDOBOOKS.COM

Printed in China.
102024
012025

Cover Photo: Roberto Machado Noa/LightRocket/Getty Images (front); Shutterstock Images (back)
Interior Photos: Roberto Machado Noa/LightRocket/Getty Images, 1; Anna Barclay/Getty Images, 5; Jerritt Clark/Getty Images for McDonald's/Getty Images, 9; Michael Siluk/Education Images/Universal Images Group/Getty Images, 12; Photo12/Universal Images Group/Getty Images, 15; The Print Collector/Heritage Images/Getty Images, 17; Transcendental Graphics/Getty Images, 23; Bettmann/Getty Images, 24; Darryl Brooks/Shutterstock Images, 29; Felix Geringswald/Shutterstock Images, 32 (top left); Shutterstock Images, 32 (top), 32 (bottom right), 67, 77; Keith Homan/Shutterstock Images, 32 (top right), 32 (bottom left), 32 (bottom); John Croft/Star Tribune/Getty Images, 34; Jeffrey Greenberg/Universal Images Group/Getty Images, 38–39; Jerry André/ATPImages/Getty Images, 41; Smith Collection/Gado/Getty Images, 43, 64; Charly Triballeau/AFP/Getty Images, 47; Jeffrey Greenberg/Education Images/Universal Images Group/Getty Images, 51; Elijah Nouvelage/AFP/Getty Images, 52; M. Phillips/WireImage/Getty Images, 55; Felipe Sanchez/Shutterstock Images, 58; David Parry/PA Wire/AP Images, 61; Jerod Harris/Getty Images for Netflix/Getty Images, 63; Ekaterina Minaeva/Shutterstock Images, 71; Pat Greenhouse/The Boston Globe/Getty Images, 74; Paul J. Richards/AFP/Getty Images, 80; James Leynse/Corbis/Getty Images, 83; Robert Daemmrich Photography Inc./Corbis Historical/Getty Images, 89; Justin Sullivan/Getty Images, 91; Clint Austin/Shutterstock Images, 92–93; David Paul Morris/Getty Images, 98

Editor: Arnold Ringstad
Series Designer: Maggie Villaume

Library of Congress Control Number: 2024938298

PUBLISHER'S CATALOGING-IN-PUBLICATION DATA
Names: Waldendorf, Kurt, author.
Title: Food marketing / by Kurt Waldendorf
Description: Minneapolis, Minnesota: ABDO Publishing, 2025 | Series: Fascinating food | Includes online resources and index.
Identifiers: ISBN 9781098295288 (lib. bdg.) | ISBN 9798384916284 (ebook)
Subjects: LCSH: Food in mass media--Juvenile literature. | Food in popular culture--Juvenile literature. | Food--Social aspects--Juvenile literature. | Advertising--Food--Juvenile literature. | Food trade--Juvenile literature. | Advertising--Food service--Juvenile literature. | Selling--Food--Juvenile literature.
Classification: DDC 338.13--dc23

CONTENTS

ATTENTION-GRABBING ADS

In early 2023, the fast food giant McDonald's rolled out an eyebrow-raising television ad. The commercial begins with a young woman delivering paperwork in a busy office. As she walks, her jaunty steps fall in rhythm to Yello's 1985 hit song "Oh Yeah."

The woman drops a thick folder onto a desk, and an employee sighs. Then inspiration strikes. With a waggle of her eyebrow, the employee scribbles a note. A moment later, she presents a drawing of the world-famous McDonald's golden arches to a coworker.

In response, the coworker nods and packs up her things, and the two begin walking rhythmically toward the exit. As they go, they raise their eyebrows, silently inviting others to join. Before long, managers, secretaries, delivery people, and

The golden arches of McDonald's were originally part
of the restaurant's architecture before becoming an

maintenance personnel are shoving aside their work and parading out of the building for their lunch breaks. At the end of the commercial, the single line of text "Fancy a McDonalds?" appears on the screen, followed by the double-arches logo, which rises and falls to the beat.

Throughout the "Raise Your Arches" ad, no steamy burgers or glistening French fries appear. No information about the company's products is given, and, other than a single line of text, no words are used. Despite all this, the commercial was a significant success. "Raise Your Arches" content trended on the social media app TikTok, inspiring more than 2.5 million pieces of user-created content.[1] The ad achieved an exceptional spike rating, a measure for short-term sales growth.

Because no words were spoken, the ad could easily be shown around the world. In the weeks after the ad's original appearance in the United Kingdom, it was shown in 35 countries. The commercial eventually racked up more than 100 million views across all platforms where it appeared.[2]

REFRESHING A GLOBAL BRAND

Since the 1950s, McDonald's has consistently used marketing to update its image, allowing it to cement its position as the world's most valuable fast food company. The "Raise Your Arches" campaign was part of McDonald's marketers' latest attempt to boost the chain's popularity with younger generations. A 2016 memo reported that only 20 percent of millennials, or people born between 1981 and 1996, had tried a Big Mac, the company's flagship burger.[4] With Gen Z, or people born between 1997 and 2012, the trend was continuing. Teens were increasingly choosing competitors such as Chick-fil-A, Chipotle, and Dunkin'.

How does an ad with no McDonald's products make the restaurant more appealing to young people?

Unlike little-known businesses that need to educate potential customers about their products, McDonald's and its products are well recognized. To have continued success, the company is focused on improving its brand, or the associations people have with the company. As one McDonald's marketer put it, "McDonald's isn't just in the business of making burgers; it's now in the business of making culture."[5] In the case of the "Raise Your Arches" ad, this meant reminding young adults, particularly millennials, of the joy and excitement that can come with an escape to the golden arches.

With Gen Z, McDonald's has found other ways to make the brand culturally relevant. In 2020 it launched its Famous Orders campaign, allowing customers to place the same orders as celebrities such as rapper Travis Scott

Rapper Saweetie showed off her signature McDonald's order at a press event in 2021.

(a Quarter Pounder with cheese, bacon, and lettuce, fries dipped in BBQ sauce, and a Sprite) and pop group BTS (chicken nuggets, fries, sweet chili and Cajun dipping sauces, and a Coke). Across social media, the company engaged customers to create their own "menu hacks," or favorite ways of combining McDonald's food items. Due in part to these efforts to re-engage young people, company sales increased nearly 6 percent in 2022.[7]

BEYOND THE SCREEN

Television ads are among the most visible ways people interact with food companies on a day-to-day basis. But food marketers go far beyond TV screens to get consumers' attention. Companies sponsor sporting events and put their names on stadiums. They post ads on billboards, in buses and trains, and on websites. They pay influencers to feature their products on social media, and they make deals with film studios to have their products appear in movies. In schools, they sponsor fundraising efforts and put branding on vending machines. In 2022 companies spent more than $16 billion on food advertising in the United States alone.[8]

Despite the enormous amount companies spend on advertising, it's only one part of the food marketing process. Long before ads appear in public, food marketers work to develop new products that will appeal to consumers. They establish prices that are competitive and will allow the company to profit. They decide where the products will be available and how they will be packaged. Finally, they create messaging strategies that let people know what the product or brand has to offer. These different parts of the marketing process are known as the four Ps: product, price, place, and promotion. For companies to be successful, they must consider each carefully.

WHY FOOD MARKETING MATTERS

For consumers, the daily flood of marketing messages they receive can make food decisions feel overwhelming. However, if taken to the opposite extreme—if no food promotion occurred and no labels appeared on food products—it would be impossible for consumers to make informed decisions. At its best, food marketing provides people with products they want and the necessary messaging to find them, leading to a higher quality of life. In return, food companies receive revenue, which can help create jobs and benefit the economy. In this way, food marketing can benefit everyone involved.

Food marketing can be beneficial in other ways too. Nonprofits, government organizations, and companies can take part in social marketing, or initiatives aimed at achieving broader benefits. Examples of social marketing

Billboards along busy roadways can expose millions of people to food marketing messages.

include programs to teach children about healthy diets or programs to keep food from going to waste. In social marketing, success is measured by the benefits to society as a whole.

However, food marketing can also have negative effects. Critics point to the fact that the food industry's main goal is to increase profit. This encourages companies to create products that can be made for less money. Often the resulting products are poor in healthy nutrients and rich in unhealthy sugars, salts, and fats. Each year, roughly 20,000 new products are introduced to US food stores. Roughly half are candy, gum, snacks, and beverages.[10]

In addition, food marketers can go wrong by using unethical messaging. This includes using misleading claims about products' benefits. It also includes targeting specific vulnerable audiences, such as marketing cheap, nutrient-poor foods to low-income communities or marketing unhealthy or addictive foods to children. Besides recognizing long-term health effects on consumers, the public is also becoming increasingly concerned about the negative effects food companies can have on the environment.

By better understanding how and why food companies create, price, distribute, and promote products, people can be better informed about their buying decisions. As nutritionist Marion Nestle says in her book *Food Politics*, "We do not make food choices in a vacuum. . . . We may believe that we make informed decisions about food choice, but we cannot do so if we are oblivious of the ways food companies influence our choices."[11]

Learning about food marketing can also help people advocate for changes they'd like to see companies make in the future. Just as McDonald's needed to revise its marketing to appeal to younger generations, if people demand practices that align with their beliefs, food marketers will have to respond to remain competitive. By voting with their purchases, consumers can help create a food industry that promotes healthier people and a healthier world.

CHAPTER TWO

FOOD MARKETING THROUGH HISTORY

Humans' basic food needs have largely stayed the same since ancient times. As food journalist Michael Pollan puts it, advice on what to eat can be boiled down to seven simple words: "Eat food. Not too much. Mostly plants."[1] But the types of foods marketed to Americans have changed dramatically over the past 200 years. These changes reflect broader developments across agriculture, manufacturing, technology, and culture.

In the mid-1800s, the average American diet consisted of seasonal fruits, vegetables, and grains that were grown locally. Meat was also a common staple in the United States and came from nearby ranchers or local hunters. Seafood was available on the coasts, where it could be caught and consumed quickly. In large cities such as New York, imported foods such as bananas and oranges were available,

THREE KINGDOMS.

NATURE HAS DIVIDED THE WORLD INTO THREE DISTINCT CREATIONS,

MINERAL, VEGETABLE, AND ANIMAL.

United they form the matter that constitutes the Globe and every thing that lives upon it. The Animal Kingdom depends entirely upon the other two for support and health, therefore the only medicine suited to the

CONSTITUTION OF MAN

IS COMPOSED ENTIRELY OF VEGETABLE EXTRACTS,

STAINBURN'S
VEGETABLE EXTRACT
PILLS

Being formed by a chemical reduction of all the medicinal properties that are derived from the plants and herbs given by NATURE'S SELF, are consequently the natural resistance provided for mankind against diseases of the blood, the bowels, and all other complaints that (originating therefrom) effect the *HUMAN SYSTEM*.

In this enlightened age when the advancement of science has accumulated *new truths* in every branch of knowledge, that department which relates to the prolongment of life has received a new impetus.

We no longer dig into the bowels of the earth, as our grandfathers did, for *mineral remedies* because they are now known to be *injurious and poisonous* in their tendency. But in all cases of sickness, reason and common sense point us to the *path of nature*, and we resort immediately to the Vegetable Kingdom for those herbs and plants which spring from the soil under the genial influence of heaven, and we there find in their beautiful and wonderful combination a sufficient influence of the mineral kingdom mingled by the mysterious laws of nature for the support and preservation of animal life.

STAINBURN'S PILLS

Tend to lengthen human existence because by the very process of *extraction* used in their preparation they contain nothing to irritate or weaken the system, but on the contrary their composition embraces every virtue condusive to health and strength.

FOR SALE HERE,

PRICE 25 CENTS PER BOX, WITH DIRECTIONS.

STAINBURN & CLICKENER, Proprietors,

338 BROADWAY, NEW YORK.

Entered according to the Act of Congress, in the year 1842, by J. W. STAINBURN & C. V. CLICKENER, in the Clerk's Office of the District Court for the Southern District of New York.

DEAN, PRINTER,
3 ANN STREET, N. Y.

In the mid-1800s, food advertisements looked far different from the colorful, flashy marketing of today.

but for the vast majority of people, food was grown, packaged, and consumed within a few miles of where they lived.

At the time, most regions in the United States were disconnected. It would be another half century before cars and modern roads would begin to develop, allowing food to be transported cross-country by truck. The railway system was expanding quickly, but commercial lines were still mostly regional. Within states, the population tended to be spread out. About 64 percent of US jobs were on farms in 1850, meaning most people lived in rural areas rather than in cities.[2]

The Industrial Revolution brought some changes to the ways people and products got from place to place by the mid-1800s. For instance, with the invention of the steamship, grains from the Midwest could travel by river to ports, where they could then be taken more easily to large cities on the coast. However, for the most part, food distribution remained a slow and expensive process.

Because of this, food producers competed locally. They focused on creating high-quality products with the idea that there was little need for marketing. Since producers were selling a relatively small number of goods, they looked

The growth of urban areas, such as New York City, helped change the ways people got their food.

for ways to lower costs so they could profit. At the time, stores sold goods to consumers by weighing out portions individually. Because of this, food producers viewed packaging as an unneeded expense and would deliver their products in bulk via plain sacks or crates.

CONNECTING THE COUNTRY

The first major shift in the modern American food industry occurred in the late 1800s. Following the US Civil War (1861–1865), the process of industrialization revved into high gear, completely transforming American society. New farming technologies came into use. Steam tractors gave farmers more power with which to plow their fields.

The combine harvester allowed farmers to harvest, separate, clean, and deliver grains with a single machine. Barbed wire fences made it so ranchers could let their cattle graze freely.

These advancements helped make farming and ranching more efficient. They also put a lot of people out of work. Many left rural areas to find jobs in cities. By 1900, nearly 40 percent of the US population lived in cities, up from about 15 percent in 1850.[3]

The migration into cities meant that much of the population lived far away from where food was produced. Food producers needed new ways to get their foods to people, and they had to do it safely. In the mid-1800s, foodborne illnesses such as dysentery and typhoid were among the leading causes of death in the United States. Spoilage and

FLASH FREEZING

Prior to the invention of flash freezing, foods would lose their flavors and turn mushy during the freezing process. Clarence Birdseye got the idea for flash freezing while on a trip to Canada, where he saw Inuit people fishing in extremely cold temperatures. When they caught a fish, it would quickly freeze on the ice. Birdseye started experimenting right away, flash freezing cabbage for his family. Eventually he perfected his Quick Freeze Machine. He also created a special display case to keep frozen foods from thawing. While at first consumers were skeptical of his frozen foods, the products quickly caught on. Before long, a variety of flash-frozen foods were available for purchase.

contamination were frequent problems when transporting raw meats, fruits, and vegetables. The more time foods took to reach their destinations, the more susceptible they were to developing harmful bacteria.

Advancements in technology helped food companies address these problems. During the Civil War, production of canned foods had ramped up to feed soldiers when they were away from their camps. After the war, companies such as Nestlé and Heinz used the same technology to deliver food to civilians living in cities. Canning allowed food companies to ship their products hundreds or even thousands of miles without spoiling.

Other advances followed. By the late 1800s, the science of pasteurization had been refined. Pasteurization involves heating liquids to extreme temperatures to kill harmful microorganisms. It allowed companies to prolong the shelf life of milk and other beverages so they could be sent greater distances. Another important development came in 1924, when biologist Clarence Birdseye introduced his flash-freezing machine. The machine gave companies a way to keep foods fresh after they'd been frozen. For the first time, high-quality seasonal fruits and vegetables could be enjoyed year-round.

Delivering uncontaminated food to cities was just one of the challenges food producers faced at the dawn of the 1900s. Between 1870 and 1920, the US population boomed, with 25 million immigrants coming to the country from overseas.[4] To provide food for the growing population, the food industry adopted production practices that had become common in other industries.

Meat processing began to take place in central locations such as Chicago, Illinois; Milwaukee, Wisconsin; and Kansas City, Missouri. Livestock were sent from across the country to be butchered and processed in large industrial plants. Due to the invention of refrigerated railcars in the 1860s, meat could then be distributed by train throughout the country.

Farming also underwent changes. In the early 1900s, scientists and manufacturers created ways to mass-produce ammonia, an important fertilizer. This development revolutionized the agricultural industry, eventually doubling the number of people one acre (0.4 ha) of land could feed.

With the ability to create higher quantities of food and send them greater distances, food companies began to pay more attention to how they packaged their goods. In 1890, the National Biscuit Company, now known as Nabisco, began to individually package its biscuits, becoming the first company to create a moisture barrier to preserve the crispness of its products. By the early 1900s, wooden crates and sacks were replaced by corrugated paper and shipping cartons.

The rise of packaging also presented food companies with an important opportunity: making their products look more appealing. By the early 1900s, mass production had allowed food companies to make more than enough food for the population. While this was good for consumers, for companies it meant a more competitive marketplace. They could no longer rely on food products selling themselves. Advertising became an important tool for getting consumers to choose a product, and packaging gave companies places to do it.

During this era, companies such as

QUAKER OATS, BRANDING PIONEER

In the late 1800s, Quaker had a problem. The company was able to produce exceptional amounts of oats thanks to advances in food processing, but it needed more people to sell them to. The company created a brand to help increase demand. Marketers developed an image of a smiling man in traditional Quaker clothing. Because the image was not specific to a particular food, it could be used across many products. Marketers developed a slogan, saying the oats "supply what brains and bodies require."[5] To drum up even more demand, Quaker left branded samples on people's doorsteps.

Campbell's, Coca-Cola, Hershey, Kraft, Jell-O, and Quaker developed iconic brands for their product labels. Companies found that brands helped consumers feel confident about the quality and safety of the foods they were purchasing. Companies also found that the more familiar a brand was, the more people were willing to pay for it. To spread awareness of their brands, companies began advertising their products everywhere they could, including on billboards, on posters, in newspapers, and over the radio.

SEGMENTING SOCIETY

The next big shift in the US food industry came in the years following World War II (1939–1945). Once again, American society was changing quickly. Between the end of the war and 1964, the US population exploded, with more than 76 million babies being born.[6] The postwar economy was also booming. Soldiers returned home and found jobs in factories, and government programs gave them the opportunity to buy houses.

Due to the strong economy, Americans were eager to spend. New car sales increased rapidly. With the rise of suburbs, supermarket chains expanded, and fast food chains quickly spread across the country.

QUAKER
Quaker Oats has been using the same character in its branding for well over a century.
PURE
ED

Technological advancements allowed people to buy refrigerators equipped with freezers, and the microwave became an everyday appliance in American homes. Increasingly, people prioritized food options that met their individual needs and were convenient.

In response to these societal changes, the food industry underwent a transformation of its own. Large food companies merged and merged again, leading to the rise of Big Food, or an industry made up of companies with concentrated market power. Big Food companies used their power to influence suppliers. For example, McDonald's was better able to control the type and size of the potatoes used to make its French fries. Coca-Cola used its clout to better control how its bottles were made.

With more control over the food-making process, Big Food companies were able to make more consistent products. Additionally, they were able to create subtle variations of their products, which they could then package and promote differently to meet the needs of different groups.

The ability to segment, or divide up, the population into distinct groups ushered in a major shift in the food industry. It gave consumers ways to find food options that were more tailored to their needs. For companies, it opened up vast new audiences for existing and new products. To take advantage of these opportunities, companies shifted their focus to understanding the wants and needs of their consumers. Food marketers took on a larger role, and modern food marketing began.

A NEW ERA

Today, societal changes continue to shape consumers' food needs and preferences. In previous generations, preservatives that had prolonged the shelf life of foods were seen as useful developments. But now, with advances in food science, people are increasingly wary of artificial ingredients such as preservatives.

Similarly, industrial food practices that were once viewed as a beneficial way of feeding a growing population are now questioned for their effects on animals and the environment. At the same time, having grown up flooded with food ads, new generations are more skeptical of the messaging from Big Food brands. Meanwhile, today's consumers continue to desire convenience. With online

ordering and speedy delivery services, consumers are
looking for their food to be increasingly accessible.

Just as in previous generations, successful food
companies have started to adapt to such social changes.
One way they've done so is by collecting data. From
supermarkets, companies receive detailed information on
how their products perform. Online, marketers see which
messages lead people to add products to their digital
shopping carts. Social media gives companies ways to gauge
people's attitudes and buying habits. Food companies
use this data not only to create targeted advertising but
also to develop new ideas, set prices, and deliver products
to shelves.

CHAPTER THREE

MEETING A NEED

Each year, food giant Coca-Cola spends more than $4 billion on advertising its products around the world.[1] With such a massive budget, it can seem as though companies such as Coca-Cola have endless money to spend on making their products successful. However, if new products don't appeal to consumers, no amount of money will help—even for companies as large as Coca-Cola.

Out of every 100 new food products launched in the United States, about 80 will fail. Developing new products is a lengthy process, taking an average of two years.[2] Food marketers must carefully consider how to invest their time and money.

When deciding where to focus their attention, food marketers choose among four categories. The lowest-risk option for companies is to try to improve sales of an existing product. In Coca-Cola's

Even brands that are already successful and world-famous, such as Coca-Cola, spend heavily on marketing.

case, it does this each year during the holiday season. The company dresses up the design of its red can in an effort to boost its flagship soda. By including Santa Claus or other holiday-themed imagery on its cans, the company aims to link the joy and excitement of the holidays with buying Coca-Cola.

The second option food marketers consider is to introduce a new product into an established market. This strategy comes with more risk, and in the case of Coca-Cola, it has had mixed results. Cherry Coke, a new flavor introduced to the soft drink market in 1985, is still on shelves today. However, other attempts, including an orange-vanilla Coke and two coffee-flavored Cokes, failed to catch on and were quickly discontinued.

The third option is to put an existing product into a new market. With Coca-Cola, for many years Diet Coke had been a popular product with women. Then, in 2005, the company decided to try to develop a new market: diet soft drinks for men. Coke Zero used nearly the same formula as Diet Coke. However, the new beverage's sleek black can and the word *zero* instead of *diet* made the product a hit with its intended audience.

The final way companies create new products is through diversification, or introducing a new product into a new market. Coke diversified in 2007, spending a whopping $4.1 billion to acquire Glacéau, the maker of the flavored water product Vitaminwater.[4] While diversification is the riskiest option, it can help companies become more stable over time. In the case of Coke, entering the fledgling health-drink market allowed the company to make up for lost sales in the 2010s as people turned away from sugary sodas.

MAKING SOMETHING UNIQUE

No matter the type of product a company chooses to create, development begins with generating ideas. When generating ideas, marketers consider how the product will provide value to consumers. In food marketing, value is the overall benefit a product provides. When measuring value, marketers consider benefits such as health, taste, convenience, and sustainability.

However, value is subjective. What one person finds tasty, another might dislike. Introducing a new flavor can

A VARIETY OF BRANDS

Major food companies, such as the Coca-Cola Company, often own many smaller brands. Each of these companies has its own marketing strategies, giving the parent company many ways to reach new groups of customers. These are just a few of the brands under the Coca-Cola umbrella.

set a product apart, but something significantly different from past products may catch consumers off guard. A 2008 food study showed that when it comes to food, people don't like surprises. The study presented participants with an unmarked, pink-colored ice cream. Because of the ice cream's appearance, participants were expecting a sweet flavor, such as cherry, strawberry, or cotton candy. But what they tasted wasn't sweet at all: it was smoked salmon. Because the savory flavor was so different from what the audience expected in an ice cream, the food earned poor reviews.

When thinking about a product's value, marketers also consider trade-offs, or things that may make people value it less. For example, a product may distinguish itself by offering health benefits, but if it's less tasty than other options, consumers may not be willing to stick with it. McDonald's learned this lesson in 1991 when it marketed a healthier alternative to the Big Mac.

The McLean Deluxe boasted 75 percent less fat than the company's best-selling burger.[5] Its patty included seaweed-based ingredients. McDonald's advertised the burger as having the same taste as a normal burger, but when the McLean Deluxe found its way onto the menu, people rejected both the taste and the burger's higher price. The burger was off the menu by 1996.

The McLean Deluxe is one of many new food products that marketers were unable to successfully sell to potential customers.

Another trade-off marketers consider is hassle. If a product is difficult to eat or requires particular equipment to prepare, people may opt for other products. For example, someone may value the taste of chocolate, but if the food melts easily and the person needs to wash their hands afterward, they likely won't pick up the product again. This was the issue Mars was looking to address when it introduced M&Ms in the 1940s. The company used a crispy sugar coating to keep the chocolates from melting. The selling point of convenience was summed up in their slogan: "It melts in your mouth, not in your hand."[6]

BRANDS

In a market in which competing food products are often similar in recipe, taste, and look, often a product's brand is what sets it apart. Brands can add value to consumers' lives by making food decisions more convenient. Most Americans' food decisions are low involvement, meaning the person making the decision might not even be aware of it.

When making low-involvement decisions, people's brains prioritize high-visibility cues that are easy to understand. If there are no clear differences between products, brands provide those cues. They allow consumers to make decisions quickly and reliably, saving time and effort.

Food brands are powerful. Experiments show that blind taste tests deliver completely different results from taste tests in which participants are aware of the brands they're trying. Over time people may develop brand loyalty, meaning they will tend to choose a particular brand if

PEPSI CHALLENGE

In 1975 Pepsi developed a bold ad campaign challenging its rival Coke directly. The Pepsi Challenge asked everyday Americans to blind taste test the two sodas and respond with which they preferred. According to the ads, Pepsi was the clear winner. However, the challenge may have given Pepsi unfair advantages. Pepsi contains more sugar, so while people might have liked the smaller amount given in the challenge, they might have been less satisfied with a full can. Nonetheless, Pepsi's ads created the perception that its product was superior, boosting its brand.

WHAT'S IN A NAME?

During World War II, chocolatiers in Turin, Italy, were cut off from their supply of cocoa. As a result, they began using hazelnut and sugar along with their limited amount of available cocoa. Eventually, they created a spreadable form of the new product, which people began using on toast. Nutella was born. As Nutella made its way through Europe and the United States, it became synonymous with nut-chocolate spreads. Like the terms Popsicle and TV dinner, Nutella not only launched a brand but also became the go-to name for an entire category of food.

it's available. Strong brand loyalty may even cause people to stick with a brand despite trade-offs, such as higher prices.

Because of these dynamics, food companies work hard to create and maintain their brands. But strong brands do not develop overnight. They develop as individual products establish trust with consumers. For companies looking to develop strong brands, the first step is making a product that meets consumers' needs.

UNDERSTANDING AN AUDIENCE

Food marketers dramatically improve the chance of a new product catching on by targeting audiences that are open to the advantages their products provide. To identify these groups, food marketers create personas, or profiles of potential buyers. These personas take into account people's eating habits, buying preferences, cooking skills, opinions, values, and emotions. Personas allow food marketers to get into the mindset of potential customers to anticipate their needs. Personas can also be used to identify the right group to approach with an existing idea.

Aside from their target audience, marketers also consider how open the general public will be to their product. For this, they group the population into five categories. Those most willing to try new products are the Innovators, who make up about 2.5 percent of the population. The Early Adopters make up about 13.5 percent and consist of people who don't want to miss a trend and will also seek out innovations. Next comes the Early Majority, at 34 percent. This group is open to new products but may not seek them out.

NESPRESSO

In 1986 Nestlé introduced a product designed for a very particular audience. At the time, getting a shot of espresso was a hassle, involving a trip to a local espresso bar. Nestlé's at-home Nespresso machines provided the convenience of creating espresso at home. The product targeted an audience known as DINKs, or adults with dual income and no kids. This audience had money to spend on the expensive machine, and they were more likely to crave a convenient coffee solution. Today, the market for the espresso pods used in the machines has exploded, with around 14 billion Nespresso capsules sold each year.[7]

Supermarkets offer a variety of products ranging from longtime brands that customers trust to innovative products that might appeal to more adventurous shoppers.

The remaining groups are the Late Majority (34 percent) and the Laggards (16 percent), the slowest groups to try new products.[8] For especially innovative products, such as chocolate-covered mealworms, marketers focus on reaching out to Innovators in hopes of starting a trend that will spread to other groups. For smaller innovations, such as salted-caramel pudding, marketers may choose to focus on larger groups right away.

After a product and audience have been identified, food marketers move on to screening for feasibility. In this process, they make sure they can deliver. They work with food scientists to create an ideal version of the food in a laboratory. They then get feedback from their manufacturing and legal teams to make sure the product will meet guidelines set up by the Food and Drug Administration (FDA). Based on this feedback, they adjust the formula so that it is safe and able to be produced in large quantities.

Once a product passes these steps, companies scale up production, and the food undergoes tests with consumers. In sensory acceptance tests, participants are asked to rate specific attributes of the food, such as flavor, appearance, and texture. Marketers also use overall-difference tests, in which the product is compared with foods already on the market.

Marketers take feedback from these tests and work with food scientists to address specific concerns. Sometimes, the product does not test well and is dropped altogether. If a product makes it through this stage, it moves into commercialization. This involves packaging the product, finalizing the costs, establishing a marketing plan, and putting the product on supermarket shelves.

Dietrich Mateschitz

Marketer Dietrich Mateschitz was on a business trip in Asia in the 1980s when he got the idea for a new product. At the time, he was working for a German company that made personal hygiene products. But when he tried an energizing drink made for truckers, he knew he had a new opportunity. The drink was called Krathing Daeng, or "Red Bull." It was unlike anything he'd tasted in Europe.

In 1987 he partnered with the company's owner. They added carbonation to the drink and changed the packaging from a glass bottle to a blue and silver can. But when they performed taste testing, the results were disappointing. A lemonade-style drink with energy boosting ingredients such as caffeine and taurine was not appealing to European tastes.

Instead of changing the drink, Mateschitz decided to develop a new market in Europe: energy drinks. He put adrenaline-fueled action at the center of the promotion campaign and invested as much as 30 percent of profits into advertising.[9] The risk paid off. At the time of Mateschitz's death in 2022, the company employed nearly 16,000 people in 175 countries. That year, more than 11.5 billion cans of Red Bull were sold worldwide.[10]

CHAPTER FOUR

HITTING THE SHELVES

Once a food company has created a product, food marketers set a price. In doing so, they consider the costs of buying, delivering, and storing ingredients, the cost of the equipment needed to make the product, and the cost of labor to pay employees. They also consider the cost of getting the product into stores.

Retailers such as supermarkets may add up to 50 percent to a product's price to pay for delivering, storing, and selling it.[1] Food marketers account for each of these things while the product is being developed to make sure the new item can be profitable. However, when setting the final price, food marketers must consider the most important variable: the consumer. For consumers, price is often a main factor in the food-buying process.

Figuring out a price that maximizes the revenue from a food product is a key challenge for marketers.

MEETING EXPECTATIONS

To determine what a fair price is, consumers think about the health benefits, taste, and convenience a food will provide. They also consider the prices of similar food options. The more competitors there are offering similar products, the likelier the person is to choose the cheapest option. Because only a few cents can be the difference in what consumers choose to buy, food marketers study their competitors closely.

Food marketers also think of how the price will affect the company's brand. Generally, consumers associate higher prices with better quality and lower prices with lower quality. Depending on how a company wants to position its brand, marketers may choose to charge more or less.

New, innovative products with few competitors can be difficult to price. For example, if a company launches a new category of snack, marketers may choose to price it like an appetizer, taking advantage of the unfamiliarity of the product to charge more. But if consumers consider the product similar to existing snacks, they may not be willing to pay a premium. For such products, companies may reach out to consumers to get feedback on how much to charge. If asked directly, most consumers underestimate how much they are willing to pay. By asking a series of questions, food marketers get better information. These questions include what price consumers think is too cheap (indicating poor quality), cheap (indicating a good deal), expensive (indicating high quality), and too expensive (out of their price range). By averaging consumers' answers to these questions, food marketers estimate an ideal price.

For small companies, it can be hard to meet consumers' price expectations. Big Food companies have large facilities, specialized technologies, and efficient supply chains, allowing them to create high volumes of food at low costs. For smaller companies, the cost of making each item may be much higher. One way for smaller companies to compete is by

PRICE GOUGING

The COVID-19 pandemic brought many disruptions to the food industry. Shipping bottlenecks slowed the movement of goods around the globe. To make up for the increased costs of delivering goods, many companies raised prices. As a result, consumers began to expect to pay more for goods across the board. Some companies saw this as an opportunity and raised their prices even if their costs hadn't gone up. This practice is known as price gouging. A 2024 report from the US Federal Trade Commission found that food companies used the pandemic "to come out ahead at the expense of their competitors and the communities they serve."[2]

using cheaper ingredients or by making changes to their supply chains. However, for companies looking to offer healthier or more sustainable foods, these changes undermine the very things that set their products apart. This dynamic can keep healthier or more sustainable options off supermarket shelves.

A COMPETITIVE MARKETPLACE

Research shows that a majority of consumers arrive at the grocery store undecided about what to buy. Supermarket managers understand this, and they collect extensive data on shoppers' decisions to better influence what people buy. As a result, everything from the way the stores are laid out to the lighting, signage, and shelving are chosen carefully.

When customers walk into a supermarket, they are often greeted by an array of sights and smells. In supermarkets that include bakeries or flower shops, these features appear near the entrance to provide pleasant aromas and deliver strong first impressions. Next, shoppers are guided

Attractive and colorful displays in the produce section often welcome shoppers into a supermarket.

to the produce section, where they're offered brightly colored fruits and vegetables. Along the walls, greens may glisten with water, reminding shoppers of a morning dew. These experiences are designed to put shoppers at ease, making them feel as if they are being provided with fresh, high-quality options.

Three out of every four consumers make impulse, or unplanned, purchases at the grocery store.[4] Even consumers with detailed lists and strong food preferences can be swayed into making spur-of-the-moment buys. Supermarkets take advantage of this by featuring appealing, colorful displays at the ends of aisles and tasty snacks in checkout lanes. Supermarkets also work to keep shoppers in the store for a longer time. The store might feature only one entrance and exit, making customers walk through the store before leaving. They might also include non-food services, such as banks or pharmacies, to increase consumers' time in the store and boost sales.

When designing aisles, supermarket managers think carefully about where consumers are likely to look. A product's location as well as the number of facings, or instances of a single item, heavily influence consumers' buying decisions. Products at eye level sell the best, so foods appealing to adults are placed on the middle shelves, and those aimed at children appear on lower shelves.

Within each food section, stores create planograms, or maps that lay out the most profitable arrangements. Each category includes the leading brands, which compete with one another and introduce new innovations to the category. Retailers also create their own brands, which are often cheaper and set the base price for the category.

Some food companies pay to get better positioning on shelves. But ultimately, the arrangement is guided by results. If a product does well over time, it earns better placement. If a brand fails to innovate over time, or if it suffers damage to its reputation, it may become vulnerable to being replaced.

To introduce a new product into stores, food marketers set up tastings with retailers. If the retailer decides that the food delivers what it promises, the retailer adds it to shelves for a trial. For small companies with innovative products, it can be hard to make it onto the competitive shelves of a supermarket. However, some retailers prioritize trying out new products to make their stores different from other supermarkets.

DELIVERING TO CONSUMERS

As a food makes its way onto shelves, marketers consider how available to make their product. For convenience items, or everyday products aimed at a wide audience, companies may partner with many retailers to get their products into as many hands as possible. Doing so not only makes the product more convenient for consumers but also boosts the food company's brand. For example, Coca-Cola's top priority has long been to make its products broadly accessible. Seeing a brand on the shelves in convenience stores, drugstores, and supermarkets can make consumers feel more confident the product is the best option.

However, for specialty products associated with high quality, the opposite may be true. If consumers see a product marketed as high quality in the aisles of a convenience store, it may hurt the brand's image by making it seem cheap. To avoid this reaction, companies often limit how available they make specialty products. In 2006, PepsiCo did this when introducing a line of natural snack foods and protein drinks. The company partnered exclusively with Whole Foods, a retailer associated with high-quality products. By making it seem as though customers were getting special access to the product, the company hoped it would lead them to think more highly of it.

Limiting availability also has downsides. Companies may miss out on reaching consumers who are open to the benefits their products provide. Additionally, there are signs that consumer expectations are changing. With online shopping widely popular, convenience is increasingly

Prominently displaying a product at many locations, including gas station convenience stores, means consumers encounter the brand more often.

affecting what people buy. Some data suggests that even with high-quality goods, people want to see them in as many places as possible.

For smaller companies with innovative products, limited distribution may be the only option because of the high costs of wider distribution. If the product succeeds, it may then be offered more widely. However, success also causes competition to grow. Large companies make their own versions of the product, often at cheaper prices. This can make it difficult for small companies to establish their brands.

Selling products at high-end stores, such as Whole Foods, can make the products feel more exclusive but also limit the potential audience.

One way small companies can develop their brands is by going straight to the consumer. Because placement in supermarkets is expensive, selling directly to consumers can be a better option. However, this approach also has its risks. Without placement in stores, it can be hard to spread brand awareness. Additionally, while people may be open to buying packaged beverages and snacks online, for fresh products such as fruits and vegetables, consumers may prefer to see the food up close.

Making people feel confident in the quality of the product can be a big challenge. With unrecognized brands, people may have concerns about safety. Food scandals involving questionable ingredients and dishonest nutrition claims have underlined these issues. Small companies address these concerns by including safety certifications on their packaging and websites. In addition, they may appear at street festivals and music events. These settings can put consumers at ease, making them more willing to try products they might otherwise avoid.

PINK SAUCE

In 2022 chef Veronica Shaw used TikTok to reach a new audience. She promoted Pink Sauce, a brightly colored condiment similar to ranch dressing. Shaw's videos featuring the fluorescent sauce quicky went viral, with people paying $20 to have it delivered to their homes. But when Pink Sauce buyers found errors on its label, they began to question the quality of the product—and its safety. To help instill confidence, Shaw partnered with a company called Dave's Gourmet. However, the company made significant changes to the product, and Shaw has claimed the agreement took advantage of her.

CHAPTER FIVE

SPREADING THE WORD

Companies use promotion to spread public awareness of their products. The most prominent way food companies promote their products is through advertising. But this is just one of the methods they use to spread awareness.

They also use sales promotions, such as sending out coupons, creating contests, or holding giveaways. Direct marketing, or sending out personalized messages through apps, emails, or mailings, is another part of the promotion mix. The field of public relations is involved too. This may involve partnering with well-known figures, sending out press releases, or holding special events.

When food marketers plan how to promote their products, they look to achieve four goals: gaining attention, increasing interest, creating desire, and causing action. They may focus on different goals

When rapper 50 Cent endorsed Vitaminwater, the deal included a share in the company, which eventually earned him tens of millions of dollars.

for different products. For a new product, companies might look to gain interest with catchy slogans or with messages that show how their product is different from others. For well-established products, companies focus on causing action. Fast food companies might show close-ups of mouthwatering burgers or ice-cold drinks, attempting to get customers to head to the drive-through.

Just as they do when creating the product itself, food marketers carefully consider their audience when crafting their messaging. The words, images, and sounds they use are crafted to account for consumers' age, education, income, gender, values, and opinions. Once marketers have crafted their messaging strategy, they place the message where it will have the most impact with consumers.

PRECISE PACKAGING

The vast majority of new foods deliver their messaging right on the packaging. This is known as point-of-purchase advertising, and it can be highly effective. While shoppers may come into a supermarket with a list of items to buy, these lists often include general food categories, such as milk, eggs, bread, and cheese, rather than specific brands. An estimated 70 percent of the time, consumers purchase brands they had not considered until seeing the products on the supermarket shelf.[1] Food marketers use a variety of techniques to draw in customers.

One is through color. Different colors carry symbolic meaning for consumers, which food marketers use to shape how their brands are understood. Red is attention grabbing and inviting, while blue makes people feel more at ease and trusting. Brown is used to make people more relaxed, while yellow evokes energy and happiness. White can be used to indicate lighter, low-calorie products.

Shapes also play an important role. People tend to associate curved shapes with femininity and more angular shapes with masculinity. Shapes can also express mood, with sharp triangles representing excitement and soft curves bringing to mind comfort and relaxation. Switzerland-based

Grocery stores may offer dozens of brands of breakfast cereal, each with its own branding and color scheme.

chocolate maker Toblerone uses distinct triangle-shaped packaging to remind customers of the Swiss Alps. Meanwhile, Coca-Cola's bold red color and iconic swooshing logo make the product seem like an inviting, refreshing treat.

For products aimed at children, companies create appealing characters. Cereal mascots Tony the Tiger, Toucan Sam, and the Trix Rabbit give their brands personality and are similar to the animated characters children might see on television. Even the positions of the characters are considered. Children's cereal characters generally look out from the packaging at a slight downward angle. Researchers believe this is to establish eye contact with young consumers, building trust in the brand.

Marketers also carefully consider the packaging text. Along with brand slogans, they include buzzwords to try to increase the brand's appeal. For example, companies may imply their food is nutritious with words such as *natural* or *fresh*. To appeal to an environmentally minded crowd, they may claim that the product is produced using sustainable sources. Studies show that claims such as these heavily affect consumer buying decisions.

REACHING REMOTELY

Companies with larger promotion budgets may choose to reach out to consumers in places beyond stores. Traditionally, remote advertising has taken place on TV, in movies, over the radio, and in print. Today, television advertising still makes up 75 percent of food companies' ad spending and 95 percent of fast food ad spending.[2]

But companies are also reaching out online, in video games, and even through virtual reality to promote their products.

Advertising remotely allows companies to reach audiences that may otherwise not come across their products. But it is also expensive. If the message isn't delivered effectively to the target audience, it may not be worth the company's time and money.

One way companies find their audiences is by partnering with influencers, or popular figures who can affect people's buying decisions. Influencers can be celebrities, athletes, or social media figures. Because influencers cater to particular groups, they give companies a way to reach the people most likely to buy their products. And because influencers serve as role models for their groups, partnering with them can help raise the brand's reputation.

WELCOME TO THE OREOVERSE

In 2023 Oreo took its advertising to a new frontier when it created a promotional campaign in the metaverse. Using virtual reality headsets, Oreo fans were able to access the Oreoverse, where they could interact with other fans and play Oreo-themed games. The promotion fit well with Oreo's reputation. An Oreo spokesperson explained, "Oreo is the cookie that begs to be played with, and we love to create new opportunities for our fans to connect with each other and share that playful spirit."[6]

In 2019, Heinz teamed up with singer-songwriter Ed Sheeran to help spread the company's messaging. Sheeran isn't only a celebrity with an enormous following. He's also a longtime Heinz fan with a tattoo of the company's ketchup bottle logo on his arm. According to Heinz, Sheeran's fans have long engaged with the brand on social media. By partnering with the musician, Heinz tapped into an already interested audience. The promotion was so successful the company enlisted Sheeran to help launch a new hot sauce in 2023.

To reach a broader audience, companies use viral marketing. Viral marketing encourages consumers to share information about a company's products online. It can also be used to spread awareness of new products. In 2023 Doritos used viral marketing to spread word of its new Sweet & Tangy BBQ chips. The company created the #DoritosTriangleTryout contest on TikTok, promising the winner a place in the

As part of its partnership with Ed Sheeran, Heinz auctioned off ketchup bottles decorated with Sheeran's tattoos—including his Heinz tattoo.

company's upcoming Super Bowl ad, along with a cash prize.
With the chance to appear during the country's biggest TV
event, popular social media influencers joined the challenge.

Other companies choose to focus on their core audience
with their promotion efforts. This can help repair a brand's
reputation. In 2009 Domino's desperately needed to improve
its image. The company had been serving the same style
of pizza for 50 years, and sales were drooping. A breaking
point came when a video comparing Domino's crust to
cardboard went viral. Instead of ignoring the controversy,
Domino's took it head on. In its "Pizza Turnaround" ad, it
spoke directly to its customers, acknowledging the feedback
and laying out big changes to the company's recipes. The
campaign worked, leading to five straight years of sales
growth.[7] By being honest with its core customers, Domino's
was able to reshape its image.

Finally, companies with smaller budgets looking to
create awareness may turn to guerrilla marketing to make
a splash. In guerrilla marketing, companies use surprising

JOHN LEONARD

In 1996 Pepsi launched an unconventional promotion called "Drink Pepsi, Get Stuff," which encouraged customers to collect "Pepsi Points" from their purchases and exchange them for prizes. In one TV commercial, the prizes shown included a shirt, a jacket, and—as a joke—a $23 million military jet.

But not everyone got the joke. College student John Leonard decided to take Pepsi up on its offer. Doing some math, he figured he'd need to drink 190 cans of Pepsi each day for a century to get enough points for the jet. But there was a loophole. The promotion's fine print said he could buy points for 10 cents each. To get the seven million points for the jet, he'd need $700,000.[9] So, with the help of a business partner, he sent a check for this amount to the company, expecting to receive his reward.

Because Pepsi did not have a jet to offer, the two sides went to court. In the end, a judge ruled against Leonard. While Leonard was upset at first, he moved on with his life. In 2022 a Netflix documentary series called *Pepsi, Where's My Jet?* premiered, renewing the promotion's controversy more than 25 years later.

IHOP turned its 2019 burger promotion into a major media event.

methods to drum up interest in their products. A particularly famous example is the Oscar Mayer Wienermobile, a hot dog–shaped car created in 1936 to spread the word of Oscar Mayer hot dogs through the streets of Chicago.

While guerrilla marketing often takes place in a physical location, companies also use this technique online. In 2019 the restaurant IHOP, primarily known for its pancakes, used guerrilla marketing to promote the burgers on its menu. On social media, the company changed its name to IHOb and announced it was now the International House of Burgers. After the promotion was done, the company changed its branding back to normal. According to one marketer with the company, the campaign quadrupled burger sales.[10]

WORKING TOGETHER

To get the most out of their promotion campaigns, food marketers coordinate their efforts. When a consumer considers a product at the point of purchase, marketers want to remind the shopper of all the associations they've built up through remote advertising. One example of pairing remote and point-of-purchase advertising comes from the sports drink Gatorade. Since the brand began in the 1960s, it has built its image by partnering with famous athletes including basketball great Michael Jordan, tennis star Serena Williams, soccer legend Lionel Messi, and baseball standout Bryce Harper. Often the company's ads feature these athletes coming off the court or field and taking a swig of the thirst-quenching beverage.

To better match its branding, Gatorade has continually updated its packaging. In the 1990s it moved from a stocky bottle to one with a broad top, slim middle, and wider bottom. This gave it the look of a human form, bringing to mind the athletes who appeared in Gatorade's commercials. Its slimmer design also makes it seem more portable, matching the images from ads of athletes grabbing the drink and taking quick sips. These elements work together to remind consumers of what they like about the brand as a whole.

CHOOSING HEALTHY FOODS

When deciding what to eat, many different dynamics affect Americans' decisions. People consider how the product has been promoted, how it's packaged, and how it's priced. They also consider food advice they've received from news articles and food blogs. One often overlooked factor in the food-selecting process is psychology.

Studies show that Americans generally divide foods into two categories: practical foods and pleasurable ones. Scientists think this phenomenon may be related to American culture more broadly. Americans tend to believe that to enjoy pleasurable activities, they must first do practical activities. When it comes to food, they apply a similar belief: to enjoy tasty treats, they must first eat more practical foods. As a result, when considering everyday food staples, Americans prioritize practical

Consumers think about healthy and unhealthy foods in
different ways. Marketers use this fact to guide their
advertising plans.

HEALTHY FAST FOOD?

In 2000, fast food chain Subway began a new marketing strategy: selling fast food as healthy. To accomplish this, the company featured ads following one man's journey as he lost weight eating Subway sandwiches. The campaign challenged the traditional view that fast food restaurants were an indulgent experience. The strategy paid off. Today, Subway has nearly as many locations around the world as McDonald's. However, not all the company's products are healthy. One study found that customers' orders from Subway and McDonald's delivered similar amounts of calories, sugar, and sodium.

benefits, such as health. When considering foods that are more indulgent, they prioritize taste.

Food marketers respond to this dynamic when positioning their products. For indulgent items, such as fast food or desserts, companies frame the food as a tasty reward. For example, Ghirardelli has positioned its caramel squares as a way to "Treat Yourself."[1] On the other hand, for foods that are daily staples, companies might emphasize their products' health benefits.

ASSESSING HEALTH

One way companies make a product appear healthier is by including statements about the product's benefits on its packaging. This may take the form of nutrient claims, such as saying a product is "high in calcium," or health claims such as "calcium builds strong bones."[2] Claims such as these are carefully regulated by the FDA and can assist consumers in choosing between similar products.

However, these claims do not paint a complete picture of a product's nutritional value. While a food may be high in calcium, it may also be high in other things, such as sugars, salts, or fats. By focusing on one positive aspect of a product, companies create what experts call a *health halo* for the product, or the perception that it is healthier than it actually is. Health halos can lead consumers to overestimate the benefits the item provides.

For more accurate information, many shoppers turn to food labels, which appear on the backs of the packaging. These labels were standardized in 1990 to give consumers objective facts about the amount of fats, salts, sugars, and other nutrients contained in a product. In 2020 the labels were updated to include more information, such as the amount of added sugars and whether the nutrients came from natural sources. Even still, the serving size, or amount of food the facts are based on, often varies from one product to the next. This can make it difficult to compare options.

To make matters more complicated, many of the items presented as healthy alternatives are made by the same companies that produce the less-healthy varieties. The Naked brand of juice is one example. When the company began operating in 1983, it distinguished itself by including natural ingredients over artificial flavors, added sugars, and preservatives. Then, in 2006, food giant PepsiCo purchased the company and began to change how the juice was made. In 2013 the brand was forced to remove its claim that the juices were "all natural."[3]

Today, an estimated 80 percent of grocery items are created by just a handful of companies.[4] Of these foods, 73 percent are ultra-processed.[5] Ultra-processed foods are those that contain many ingredients not found in a normal kitchen. For example, the strawberry variety of a Nutri-Grain bar contains dozens of items on the ingredient list. Other ultra-processed foods include sodas, cookies, energy bars, flavored yogurts, packaged cereals, and frozen meals. Often, these foods are high in fat, sugar, or salt and contain various artificial flavorings, dyes, and sweeteners.

DECLINING HEALTH, INCREASING PROFITS

From a food marketing perspective, it makes sense for companies to create these foods. Highly processed foods can be made in large quantities and with cheap ingredients, meaning they can be sold for more profit. Major food companies such as Kraft Heinz, General Mills, and Nestlé made an average of 17 percent profit on the highly processed foods they sold between 2019 and 2024. Over the same period, food companies that made less-processed food staples, such as meat giant Tyson, averaged only 6 percent profit on their products.[6]

Humans are naturally drawn to foods that are sweet, fatty, and high in calories. Over the course of human history, this has helped people meet their nutritional needs. But in nature, sweet foods such as berries deliver relatively little sugar and also have fiber. Fatty foods such as nuts contain a lot of fat, but it is mostly healthy fat. Today, processed foods may

Nutrition labels are designed to give clear, objective information about food products, giving consumers something other than marketing on which to base their purchasing decision.

be high in sugar and high in unhealthy fats. They may also present intense flavors and bright colors, making them hard to resist. As one evolutionary biologist has put it, "We by nature are drawn to eating, and the companies changed the food."[7]

Due in part to the high amounts of sugar, salt, and fat in highly processed foods, Americans' health has suffered. Research has found that eating ultra-processed foods puts people at a higher risk for heart disease, type 2 diabetes, anxiety, depression, and sleep problems. Defenders of highly processed foods may claim that food companies are creating foods that meet consumers' needs. After all, the foods are often affordable, convenient, and tasty. However, critics of these foods see the industry as creating demand

ADDICTIVE FOODS?

For years, scientists have debated whether to classify certain foods as addictive. Studies show that if sugars and fats are mixed in large enough quantities, they can have an effect similar to nicotine, a chemical found in cigarettes. Highly processed foods have also been shown to rewire the brain over time, creating cravings. When people stop eating these foods, they can go through withdrawal, feeling irritable and experiencing headaches. Still, some scientists are hesitant use the term *addictive* to describe these foods. They fear that if such claims are not rigorously backed up, they may be easily ignored by food companies and the public.

for products that are profitable without considering people's long-term health needs.

UNEQUAL EFFECTS

For some groups of Americans, it can be particularly hard to access healthy foods. This is the case for some Black and Hispanic communities. While there are many reasons for this disparity, food marketing plays a role. Black and Hispanic communities tend to be in concentrated areas and have high rates of media usage. This allows food companies to reach them easily with targeted advertisements. Because these communities tend to be less affluent, often the foods advertised are cheap and low quality. In 2021, 75 percent of the money spent on advertising to these communities focused on candy, sugary drinks, cereal, and snacks.[8]

In addition, grocery chains are less likely to open stores in low-income communities. This creates food deserts, or areas with limited access to high-quality foods. In Chicago, an estimated 500,000 people live in food deserts, with

Candy, sugary drinks, snacks, and cereals made up three-quarters of Black-targeted TV ad spending in 2021.[9]

another 400,000 people living in areas where grocery stores are sparse and fast food is more convenient. One study found that in Black Chicago neighborhoods, the closest grocery store was on average two times farther away than the nearest fast food restaurant.[10]

However, communities are pushing back against these problems. One way is through food cooperatives, or co-ops. Co-ops are grocery stores in which workers share ownership of the company, giving them more input into which foods make it onto shelves. Many co-ops offer programs that allow members of the community to weigh in on the company's food choices. By doing this, these grocery stores prioritize the health and happiness of their customers rather than seeking to create profit for a larger company based elsewhere.

Food hubs can also play a role in bringing more high-quality options to communities. These are organizations that help smaller producers with storage, distribution, and marketing. By pooling their goods through a food hub, these producers can more easily get them into local grocery stores, schools, hospitals, and restaurants. Nearly 40 percent of food hubs focus on increasing access to fresh foods in underserved areas.[11] By doing so, food hubs strengthen local businesses and provide communities access to healthy, affordable foods.

MANDELA GROCERY

Worker-owned cooperatives have a rich history in Black communities. One example is Mandela Grocery in Oakland, California. When the co-op started in 2009, residents of West Oakland were in a food desert. People had to take public transit to grocery stores or turn to dollar stores or fast food restaurants to meet their food needs. At Mandela, worker-owners prioritize stocking healthy, locally made foods on shelves. The organization has also offered training to launch new co-ops. In 2021, it helped start a co-op in East Oakland, another area with few fresh food options.

CHAPTER SEVEN

MARKETING TO CHILDREN

dvertising aimed at children is a controversial area of food marketing. Each year, US companies spend billions on food advertising intended for children and teens. Much of this money goes to promoting sugary drinks, cereals, sweets, and snacks. For food companies, it makes economic sense to advertise to kids. In the United States, there is an entire media ecosystem built for children, with dedicated TV channels, websites, and social media platforms designed to cater to them.

Traditionally, the main way food companies have reached children is through TV ads. These ads can have a particularly strong effect on young children. Research suggests younger children are less likely to understand the difference between ads and TV shows, blurring the line between content meant to inform or entertain and ads made to push a product.

The Trix Rabbit is one of many cartoon food mascots designed to appeal to children.

This can be particularly harmful if the ads are for unhealthy foods. According to Margo Wootan of the Center for Science in the Public Interest, some networks feature better ads than others. "Cartoon Network, Discovery Family, Nickelodeon, and Nicktoons . . . repeatedly encourage kids to eat foods and sugary drinks that promote eating habits that could harm their health," she said in 2019. "PBS, Univision, Nick Jr., and Disney are relatively free of junk-food ads."[1]

In recent years, online videos and social media platforms have become the top media sources for kids. As a result, food marketers have responded with increased ads online. These ads further blur the lines between advertising and entertainment. On websites such as Instagram and TikTok, brands often push children to make user-generated content featuring particular products. One study found that children on these platforms were often unable to tell which posts were ads and which were organic content.

The platform YouTube Kids has rules against paid food advertising. However, creators still use paid product placement and endorsements to feature unhealthy items in their videos. One study found that in the content produced by the five most-watched child YouTube influencers, more than 90 percent of the foods mentioned were unhealthy items.[3]

For younger audiences, companies may feature advergames, or games featuring branded characters, on their websites. In the case of advergames, there is no difference between entertainment and advertising. The two are combined.

Outside the home, children are exposed to food ads at school. Because children spend most of their days in school, they are a captive audience. Children may pass by a single brand logo many times in a day, making these good investments for food companies. Companies put their logos on vending machines, posters, and stadium scoreboards. They also sponsor fundraising campaigns, such as selling Hershey's chocolate bars. Sponsorships such as these help

raise money for schools. However, because teachers and school officials are authority figures and may even be seen as role models, putting food brands in schools can make children think more highly of unhealthy products.

ECONOMIC SENSE VS. COMMON SENSE

Another reason food companies advertise to kids is to better influence what their parents buy. One study found that 80 percent of parents spent more money when their children were with them at the grocery store.[4] This ability is known as pester power, and food marketers use it to their advantage.

In the fast food industry, McDonald's used this phenomenon when it introduced the Happy Meal nationally in 1979. At the time, the company was popular among adults, but it was struggling with children. With the introduction of the specially packaged meal—and the toy that came inside—kids soon became the ones driving traffic to the stores. As a result, McDonald's not only sold more burgers but also became one of the leading toy distributors in the country.

Teaming up with popular toy brands, such as in the famous Beanie Babies campaign in the late 1990s, increased the Happy Meal's popularity even more. These collectible stuffed animals were in high demand, and the promotion put miniature versions into every Happy Meal. By tapping into children's love of collecting, McDonald's saw record sales with the promotion.

As significant as pester power is, companies also market products to children for them to buy on their own. For children, buying products that are different from those their parents choose can bring a sense of independence.

Food marketers tap into this desire when positioning their products. For example, companies create products that are playful and resemble toys so that children will feel that they are getting something uniquely for them. While children's parents might never go for a Fruit Roll-Up that unravels like a yo-yo or a lollipop that turns the eater's mouth purple, for children these products offer a way to get something that is special to them.

Selling products directly to children also helps food companies reach another goal: establishing brand loyalty. By getting kids to buy a brand's products at an early age, companies can create steady buyers in the future. Research shows that creating a connection to a product early in a child's life can lead to brand biases that last long into adulthood.

While it makes economic sense for companies to promote foods to children in these ways, critics argue the practice is unethical. They claim there is a clear link between junk-food ads and children's health. Research supports this view. Studies show that unhealthy food advertising is a major contributor to poor-quality diets among children. Children with poor diets are at significantly higher risk for developing heart disease and type 2 diabetes.

Groups already targeted by television food advertising receive an extra dose of these marketing messages. One study found that Black teens viewed 119 percent more food-related TV ads than white teens.[6] To address these issues, critics of food advertising practices argue that commonsense measures need to be taken.

REGULATING THE INDUSTRY

Efforts to rein in the American food industry's marketing machine go back decades. The first outcry about its negative effects on children came in the 1970s. At the time, the average American child saw an estimated 7,000 ads for sugary foods per year.[7] Perhaps unsurprisingly, the leading childhood illness during this period was tooth decay.

The Federal Trade Commission (FTC) proposed new rules around advertising to children. The agency suggested a ban on TV ads that promoted sugary products to children

Part of the FTC's role is to protect consumers, including by stopping companies from running misleading advertisements.

ages eight to eleven. The FTC also proposed a ban on all TV ads targeting children under eight years old, with the idea that these ads were necessarily unfair and deceptive. But when the FTC brought the proposals to Congress, legislators rejected the ideas and stripped the FTC of its ability to regulate advertising to children altogether.

Instead, Congress gave the power to industries to self-regulate advertising to children. The food industry created guidelines to remove some forms of ads, such as those that encouraged children to eat excessively. For example, an ad for an online Bagel Bites giveaway that stated, "The more you scarf, the better your chances!" was considered a violation.[8] But the industry guidelines did not limit the number of food ads or the types of foods being featured.

Then, in 2003, a study established a clear link between advertising and how much children ate and drank. The study found that ads such as those for Coca-Cola not only increased how much a child drank that brand of soda but also increased the amount of sugary drinks the child drank overall. This was a turning point in how Americans saw food marketing. More calls for regulation emerged.

In 2006 the food industry responded by creating the Children's Food and Beverage Advertising Initiative (CFBAI). The CFBAI set out guidelines to limit ads for foods that did not meet certain nutritional standards. However, participation in the initiative was voluntary, meaning that companies were not forced to comply. In addition, because the food industry created the nutritional standards themselves, critics raised concerns about how effective the standards would be.

In 2009 Congress asked the FTC and other agencies to come up with new nutrition standards. The resulting standards, which were released for public comment in 2011, were much more restrictive than the ones the food companies were using. As a result of lobbying from the food industry, the guidelines were never finalized, and no federal regulations were created.

Finally, in 2020 the CFBAI implemented stricter nutrition guidelines for food ads aimed at children. It also limited the number of ads companies could show for unhealthy products. Many saw this as a step in the right direction. However, there are still loopholes.

For example, less than 10 percent of foods made by Kool-Aid, Chef Boyardee, Lunchables, Rice Krispies, and Pop-Tarts meet the health standards laid out in the CFBAI standards.[10] However, companies can still advertise these brands generally, likely leading children to choose their less-healthy options. Additionally, the rules cover only children ages 12 and under. There are no rules for children ages 12 to 17. In 2023 the World Health Organization (WHO) urged countries to do more to protect children from the negative effects of food ads, noting specifically the use of cartoons, toys, and celebrities to endorse products.

PROMOTING HEALTHY DIETS

One way people have pushed back against the negative effects of food ads is to use the power of advertising to promote healthier foods, such as fruits and vegetables. One successful example came in 2010, when onion producer Vidalia teamed up with the animated ogre character Shrek to promote its products. The result was a sales boost of 50 percent.[11]

Social marketing can also play a role. In 1991 the National Cancer Institute established a program called 5 A Day for Better Health to encourage healthier eating among children. Now known as Fruits & Veggies—More Matters, the program has been successful in getting participants to eat more fruits and vegetables per day. But because children's food advertising continues to be dominated by Big Food companies with large budgets, it can be difficult for smaller programs such as More Matters to reach a broad audience.

GETTING KIDS INVOLVED

In 2012 frozen-vegetable company Birds Eye tried a new strategy to get young people interested in healthier foods: asking kids for inspiration. The company teamed up with fans of the Nickelodeon TV show *iCarly*, asking kids to share their ideas for fun and silly veggie dishes. Of the 16,000 entries, the top recipe idea was featured in an *iCarly* episode. Star of the show Jennette McCurdy said of the program, "It's all about kids talking to kids to get each other excited about veggies. Veggies have always been cool, but now there's proof!"[12]

CHAPTER EIGHT

MARKETING A BETTER FUTURE

Consumers today aren't worried only about the long-term effects foods are having on people. They are also concerned with how their choices affect the health of the planet. One area of focus is the way in which the food industry contributes to climate change. Because the food industry is so large, it is a major source of greenhouse gases, contributing an estimated 30 percent of global emissions.[1] These emissions come from raising livestock, producing crops, transporting goods, and processing foods.

Consumers are also concerned with other practices they see as unsustainable. Food companies rely on large farms, which often grow a single type of crop. This practice allows these farmers to produce large quantities, but it also requires more fertilizer to keep fields productive. These chemicals

The food industry plays a role in many of today's
environmental concerns, including plastic waste.

SUSTAINABILITY AND PSYCHOLOGY

While research shows positive attitudes toward sustainable products have spread, it also shows these attitudes don't necessarily lead to more purchases of these items. The difference between consumers' attitudes and behavior is known as a value-action gap. For sustainable foods, some researchers think the gap is caused by consumers not expecting such foods to taste as good. Others suggest that price and taste are simply more powerful motivators for consumers.

can lead to runoff that harms the surrounding land and water. Additionally, farming a single type of crop requires more irrigation. In the United States, more than 40 percent of freshwater usage goes to agriculture.[2] An estimated 50 percent of water used for irrigation is wasted.[3]

For food marketers, creating products that speak to consumers' sustainability concerns is an opportunity for growth. One area of focus has been in finding alternatives to animal-based products such as beef, lamb, pork, and chicken, which create significant greenhouse gas emissions. Between 2018 and 2022, sales of plant-based meat alternatives more than doubled, with companies such as Beyond Meat and Impossible Foods creating popular options.[4] While sales have leveled in recent years, two-thirds of Gen Z and millennial consumers report planning to spend more on plant-based alternatives in the future.[5]

As a result, Big Food has taken notice. Kraft Heinz has introduced plant-based alternatives for its sliced cheeses, its boxed Mac & Cheese, and its Oscar Mayer hot dogs and sausages. Even meat giant Tyson has joined its competitors, adding plant-based alternatives to its offerings.

To better match the taste and texture of meat products, startup companies are experimenting with different protein substitutes, such as algae, mushrooms, and sunflowers. Startups have also made advances in cultivated meats, or those that are grown from animal cells in a lab. In 2023, Good Meat and Upside Foods became the first companies approved to sell lab-grown meat in the United States.

Companies that rely on agriculture are also taking steps to respond to consumers' environmental expectations. In an effort to make grain-dependent brands such as Cheerios and Pillsbury more sustainable, General Mills has invested in

A chef slices lab-made chicken from Good Meat. The company feeds animal cells in stainless steel tanks to produce its meat products.

regenerative agriculture. Regenerative agriculture is an approach to farming that enhances soil health, crop diversity, and water retention. In 2024, General Mills had committed about 500,000 acres (200,000 ha) to its regenerative agriculture initiative.[6] Other large food companies, including PepsiCo, Nestlé, Danone, and Unilever, have also made commitments to support regenerative agriculture.

The need to address consumers' sustainability concerns has created a wave of innovative products and approaches in the food industry. However, some companies have

been accused of taking advantage of the moment by greenwashing, or using environmental claims only to improve their image. One example came in 2024, when meat giant JBS USA Food Company was sued by the New York attorney general for misleading the public with its claims. The company had committed to reducing greenhouse gas emissions, claiming it would be "Net Zero by 2040."[7] But in 2023 the company's CEO said publicly he did not know how to calculate the company's emissions, much less have a plan to decrease them.

Today, it is easier than ever to access online information about food's impact on the environment. Consumers are increasingly able to make sure companies such as JBS are backing up their claims with action. However, Big Food companies have a number of ways to avoid following through with their promises.

BARRIERS TO CHANGE

Whether addressing concerns about the nutritional value of foods, the role of advertising on children, or the industry's effect on the environment, food companies are resistant to change. Each of these issues has the potential to affect food companies' profits. As a result, the food industry generally tries to keep doing business as usual.

One way companies insulate themselves from change is by merging together, or consolidating. One study found that in the United States, about 79 percent of pasta is created by just three companies, and nearly 50 percent of US meat is processed by four companies.[8] Companies claim that by merging they are able to create products more cheaply and therefore offer foods at lower prices. In reality, consolidation often has the opposite effect. It reduces competition, allowing companies to charge higher prices.

Consolidation also keeps innovations out of the market. If a company introduces something new, Big Food corporations can simply buy up the company.

Food companies also resist change by influencing how brands and products are discussed. One way they do this is through front groups, or organizations that appear independent but that spread messages to support the company's interests. The names of front groups often make them sound as if they are working for the public. Keep Food Affordable, the Center for Consumer Freedom, and the Bell Institute of Health and Nutrition are just some examples. However, these groups work to stop any regulation that would hurt companies' profits.

Other ways Big Food companies change the conversation include putting pressure on news organizations to keep them from reporting on

THE COST OF CONSOLIDATION

Consolidation isn't limited to Big Food companies. It also occurs with food distributors and food suppliers. Americans felt the effects of this in 2021 when Abbott, a baby formula supplier, closed a manufacturing plant due to safety concerns. Because of consolidation, just four companies were responsible for creating 99 percent of the nation's supply of baby formula. The plant that Abbott shut down was responsible for 20 percent of the supply.[9] The temporary closure led to a nationwide shortage of formula.

For food companies, it makes sense to fund research into their products. The arrangement also makes sense for scientists, who need money to do research. However, companies can affect the scientific process in a number of ways. They might set up the rules for the experiment, steering the study in one direction. They might offer to pay for scientists' travel expenses or give them speaking fees. These can unconsciously change how scientists do their work. One possible solution, proposed by nutritionist Marion Nestle, would be to create a general fund that companies pay into for food research. That way, no single company would have too much influence.

unflattering topics, lobbying government officials to influence public nutrition advice, and hiring dietitians to promote claims that support their products. Companies even shape research done by universities and other organizations by funding studies or paying researchers. One review of industry-backed scientific studies found they were more likely to produce industry-friendly conclusions than those funded by non-industry sources.

SIGNS OF PROGRESS

Despite these obstacles, progress is being made in addressing the major challenges facing the food industry. After the COVID-19 pandemic began, the US government laid out a plan to increase competition in the meat industry by providing grants to independent suppliers. In 2024, the FTC challenged a merger by grocery giants Kroger and Albertsons, two of the largest supermarket chains in the United States. The FTC is also investigating food companies such as Kraft and Tyson for unfairly raising prices during the pandemic. These steps signal an awareness of negative effects of consolidation on the food industry.

On the topic of ultra-processed foods, there are also signs of change. Starting in 2025, the US Departments of Health and Human Services (HHS) and Agriculture (USDA) planned to study the connection between highly processed foods and health problems. Additionally, in 2024 HHS promoted a program called Food Is Medicine, which aims to address food insecurity, reduce nutrition-related diseases, and increase awareness of a healthy diet.

As part of Food Is Medicine programs, supermarkets employ registered dietitians to provide personalized nutrition counseling. This one-to-one approach helps

Some countries limit marketing toward children, including using toys to promote food to kids.

consumers cut through the noise of advertising and find foods tailored to their health needs.

Finally, while loopholes remain in US policies on advertising foods to children, in 2023, President Joe Biden called for a ban on targeted ads aimed at children online. Globally, countries such as the United Kingdom, Ireland, Chile, and Mexico have taken additional steps, such as banning TV ads for foods high in fats, sugars, or salts, banning the use of cartoon characters, celebrities, and toys in promotions aimed at children, and limiting the time of day that TV ads for unhealthy foods can be shown. In 2023, Norway became the first country to ban ads for unhealthy foods targeted at children altogether.

SENDING A MESSAGE

Throughout the history of the US food industry, companies have responded to the ways in which society has changed. Today, the food industry is also adapting to a changing planet. For food companies to navigate this shift successfully, they must continue to listen to the needs of Americans. For consumers, better understanding how foods are produced and marketed can help them make food decisions that represent their values.

Consumers can also go beyond voting with their purchases. The label of every US food product has contact information, allowing people to tell companies their thoughts directly. Many food brands are also on social media, opening another avenue for feedback.

People can push for change in other ways, too, such as advocating for further research into the connections between food and health. They can push for policies or regulations they'd like to see the government put in place. Marion Nestle explains in her book *Unsavory Truth*, "As citizens, we need and deserve healthier, more sustainable, and more ethical food systems. If we do not demand them, who will?" [11]

FOOD MARKETING BASICS

- Food marketing can be helpful to both consumers and companies. It can provide foods that meet people's needs, create profits for companies, and help strengthen the economy.

- By understanding food marketing, consumers can better see how they are being influenced.

- Often, the only noticeable difference between two competitive products is branding. Because of this, companies work hard to establish brand loyalty.

- Promotion for most food products takes place on the product itself. These point-of-purchase ads are designed to make consumers remember other ads they've seen in the past.

FOOD MARKETING HISTORY

- The food industry in the United States has changed rapidly over the past 200 years. These changes reflect advances in technology as well as changes in US culture.

- Modern food marketing began when the supply of food more than met the demand. To gain an advantage, companies focused on understanding what consumers wanted.

INTRODUCING NEW FOODS

- Food marketers seek to create products that add value to people's lives. Value may be measured by the taste, healthiness, and convenience of the item.

- Products go through extensive testing before ever reaching shelves. This includes testing for safety, taste, and the feasibility of mass production.

- Because new products compete with items from major established companies, it can be difficult for those products to reach store shelves.

ISSUES AND CONTROVERSIES

- Most new products that major food companies create are ultra-processed. These products are particularly aimed at low-income communities and children.

- The food industry self-regulates when it comes to advertising for children. Food companies have lobbied Congress to avoid stronger regulations.

- Dynamics such as consolidation, front groups, and the funding of scientific studies have helped insulate major food companies from change.

- The US food industry is in the midst of a new shift as climate change and population growth continue. As in the past, the industry must respond to consumers' changing desires.

QUOTE

"We do not make food choices in a vacuum. . . . We may believe that we make informed decisions about food choice, but we cannot do so if we are oblivious of the ways food companies influence our choices."

—*Marion Nestle, author of the book* Food Politics

affluent
Wealthy.

concentrated
Contained in a small area.

diabetes
A health condition caused by a lack of the hormone insulin, leading to high levels of sugar in the blood and urine.

dietitian
An expert in nutrition.

flagship
The finest, largest, or most important of a group of products.

food insecurity
The state of being unable to consistently access or afford adequate food.

industrialization
The transformation of the economy of a nation from a focus on farming to a focus on manufacturing.

lobbying
Attempting to influence or sway public officials toward a desired action.

market
To promote a product or service to encourage customers to purchase it.

microorganism
A living thing too small to be seen with the naked eye.

pandemic
The outbreak of disease over a large area.

preservative
A substance added to food to keep it from spoiling.

processed
Of food and ingredients, having been changed from a natural
state through a special treatment.

regulate
To create authoritative rules that guide procedures or practices.

subjective
Peculiar to a particular individual and affected by personal views,
experience, or background.

subtle
Small in scale or difficult to perceive.

suburb
A smaller community within commuting distance of a city.

supply chain
The companies, materials, and systems involved in
manufacturing and delivering a type of good.

SELECTED BIBLIOGRAPHY

Moss, Michael. *Hooked*. Random House, 2021.

Neff, Roni. *Introduction to the US Food System: Public Health, Environment, and Equity.* Jossey-Bass & Pfeiffer, 2014.

Nestle, Marion. *Unsavory Truth: How Food Companies Skew the Science of What We Eat.* Basic Books, 2018.

FURTHER READINGS

Lond-Caulk, Tina. *Eat Well and Feel Great*. Bloomsbury, 2023.

Mahoney, Ellen. *Food Stars: 15 Women Stirring Up the Food Industry.* Chicago Review, 2023.

Sonneborn, Liz. *How Supermarkets Work*. Abdo, 2025.

ONLINE RESOURCES

To learn more about food marketing, please visit **abdobooklinks.com** or scan this QR code. These links are routinely monitored and updated to provide the most current information available.

For more information on this subject, contact or visit the following organizations:

DR PEPPER MUSEUM
300 S. 5th St.
Waco, TX 76701
drpeppermuseum.com
help@drpeppermuseum.com

Dr Pepper was first manufactured and sold in the United States beginning in 1885. This museum educates and entertains the general public through the preservation, interpretation, collection, and exhibition of objects related to the history of the soft drink industry.

GRIFFIN MUSEUM OF SCIENCE AND INDUSTRY
5700 S. DuSable Lake Shore Dr.
Chicago, IL 60637
msichicago.org

The Farm Tech exhibit in the Griffin Museum of Science and Industry takes visitors through the ways in which the farm industry has adapted to meet the country's food needs.

SPAM MUSEUM
101 3rd Ave. NE
Austin, MN 55912
spam.com/museum

The Spam Museum is dedicated to the popular canned meat product that has been found on store shelves since the 1930s. The free museum features advertisements from throughout Spam's history.

SOURCE NOTES

CHAPTER 1. ATTENTION-GRABBING ADS

1. Michaela Jefferson. "McDonald's Achieves 'Exceptional' Branding Score with Eyebrow Raising Ad." *Marketing Week*, 16 Jan. 2023, marketingweek.com. Accessed 3 July 2024.
2. "Raise Your Arches." *Leo Burnett*, 26 Oct. 2023, leoburnett.co.uk. Accessed 3 July 2024.
3. Jaylen Heady. "How Many McDonald's Restaurants Are There in the World?" *Yahoo! Finance*, 20 Apr. 2024, finance.yahoo.com. Accessed 3 July 2024.
4. Julie Jargon. "McDonald's Turns to Social Media to Draw Millennials." *Wall Street Journal*, 13 Oct. 2016, wsj.com. Accessed 20 Mar. 2024.
5. Rebecca Stewart. "Golden Arch-itects." *Adweek*, vol. 44, no. 4, Apr. 2023. 18.
6. Terry O'Reilly. "This Burger Chain Showed Mouldy Food in Its Advertising." *CBC*, 26 May 2022, cbc.ca. Accessed 3 July 2024.
7. Stewart, "Golden Arch-itects," 20.
8. Julia Faria. "Topic: Food Advertising." *Statista*, 18 Dec. 2023, statista.com. Accessed 3 July 2024.
9. Aimee Picchi. "How Much Do Super Bowl Commercials Cost for the 2024 Broadcast?" *CBS News*, 11 Feb. 2024, cbsnews.com. Accessed 3 July 2024.
10. "Food Marketing and Labeling." *Johns Hopkins Center for a Livable Future*, 9 June 2017, foodsystemprimer.org. Accessed 3 July 2024.
11. Marion Nestle. *Food Politics: How the Food Industry Influences Nutrition and Health.* University of California Press, 2007. 360.

CHAPTER 2. FOOD MARKETING THROUGH HISTORY

1. Michael Pollan. "Unhappy Meals—Michael Pollan." *New York Times*, 28 Jan. 2007, nytimes.com. Accessed 18 Apr. 2024.
2. "Farm Population Lowest Since 1850s." *New York Times*, 20 July 1988, nytimes.com. Accessed 18 Apr. 2024.
3. Jonathan Rees. "Industrialization and Urbanization in the United States, 1880–1929." *Oxford Research Encyclopedia of American History*, 7 July 2016, oxfordre.com. Accessed 18 Apr. 2024.
4. Joseph Locke and Ben Wright. "18. Life in Industrial America." *American Yawp*, 22 Jan. 2019, americanyawp.com. Accessed 18 Apr. 2024.
5. Roni Neff. *Introduction to the US Food System.* Jossey-Bass & Pfeiffer, 2014. 248.
6. Kelvin Pollard and Paola Scommegna. "Just How Many Baby Boomers Are There?" *Population Reference Bureau*, 16 Apr. 2014, prb.org. Accessed 3 July 2024.
7. "How Highly Processed Foods Liberated 1950s Housewives." *National Women's History Museum*, 11 May 2017, womenshistory.org. Accessed 18 Apr. 2024.

CHAPTER 3. MEETING A NEED

1. Jan Conway. "Coca-Cola Co.: Ad Spend 2018." *Statista*, 2023, statista.com. Accessed 18 Apr. 2024.

2. Marc Emmer. "95 Percent of New Products Fail. Here Are 6 Steps to Make Sure Yours Don't." *Inc.*, 6 July 2018, inc.com. Accessed 18 Apr. 2024.

3. "Coca-Cola Market Capitalization." *Companies Market Cap*, 2024, companiesmarketcap.com. Accessed 9 May 2024.

4. "Coca-Cola to Buy Glaceau for $4.1 Billion." *Reuters*, 9 Aug. 2007, reuters.com. Accessed 18 Apr. 2024.

5. Madeline Gibson et al. "Food Marketing." *Darden Business Publishing*, 27 Aug. 2018, papers.ssrn.com. Accessed 3 July 2024.

6. "M&Ms." *Museum of Modern Art*, n.d., moma.org. Accessed 3 July 2024.

7. Dennis Limmer. "The Rise and Sustainability of Coffee Nespresso Pods." *Retail Wire*, 27 July 2023, retailwire.com. Accessed 18 Apr. 2024.

8. Bard Wernaart and Bernd van der Meulen. *Applied Food Science*. Wageningen Academic Publishers, 2022. 466.

9. Kerry A. Dolan. "Billionaire Red Bull Founder Dietrich Mateschitz Dies at Age 78." *Forbes*, 23 Oct. 2022, forbes.com. Accessed 18 Apr. 2024.

10. "Red Bull Sells Almost 11.6 Billion Cans in 2022." *Metal Packager*, 25 Jan. 2023, metalpackager.com. Accessed 18 Apr. 2024.

CHAPTER 4. HITTING THE SHELVES

1. Bart Wernaart and Bernd van der Meulen. *Applied Food Science*. Wageningen Academic Publishers, 2022. 470.

2. Christine Blank. "US FTC Accuses Retailers of Price-Gouging." *Seafood Source*, 25 Mar. 2024, seafoodsource.com. Accessed 18 Apr. 2024.

3. Brian Wansink. "Food Marketing." *Social Science Research Network*, 21 June 2003, papers.ssrn.com. Accessed 18 Apr. 2024.

4. "Psychology of the Grocery Store." *USC Applied Psychology Degree*, 17 Nov. 2023, appliedpsychologydegree.usc.edu. Accessed 18 Apr. 2024.

CHAPTER 5. SPREADING THE WORD

1. Brian Wansink. "Food Marketing." *Social Science Research Network*, 21 June 2003, papers.ssrn.com. Accessed 18 Apr. 2024.

2. Mary Story and Simone French. "Food Advertising and Marketing Directed at Children and Adolescents in the US." *International Journal of Behavioral Nutrition and Physical Activity*, vol. 1, no. 1, 10 Feb. 2004. 3.

3. "Arby's® Unveils Brand Re-Launch and New Advertising Campaign: 'Slicing Up the Truth about Freshness.'" *CNBC*, 1 Oct. 2012, cnbc.com. Accessed 9 May 2024.

4. Melanie Warner. "Wendy's Natural Cut Fries: Better Tasting, Yes. Natural, No." *CBS News*, 16 Apr. 2011, cbsnews.com. Accessed 9 May 2024.

5. "Enjoy a Flavor-Cation with New HI- CHEW™ Açaí and Tropical Mix." *Hi-Chew*, 4 May 2018, hi-chew.com. Accessed 9 May 2024.

6. "The Oreo Brand's Most Playful Cookie Ever Twists Open the Most Playful World Ever." *PR Newswire*, 24 Jan. 2023, prnewswire.com. Accessed 18 Apr. 2024.

7. "Case Study: How Domino's and Crispin Porter & Bogusky Transformed the Pizza Chain into a Tech Company." *Campaign Live*, 15 Feb. 2017, campaignlive.com. Accessed 18 Apr. 2024.

8. Brittany Hodak. "Ed Sheeran's $1,800 Ketchup Bottle." *Forbes*, 9 Aug. 2019, forbes.com. Accessed 18 Apr. 2024.

9. Joy Saha. "The 7 Most Bizarre 'Pepsi, Where's My Jet?' Revelations from Netflix's Strange-but-True Docuseries." *Salon*, 19 Nov. 2022, salon.com. Accessed 6 July 2024.

10. Amelia Lucas. "IHOP's Fake Name Change Helped It Sell 4 Times More Burgers." *CNBC*, 7 Feb. 2019, cnbc.com. Accessed 18 Apr. 2024.

CHAPTER 6. CHOOSING HEALTHY FOODS

1. "Ghirardelli Caramel Squares TV Spot, 'Treat Yourself.'" *iSpot.tv*, 25 Sept. 2023, ispot.tv. Accessed 6 July 2024.

2. "Label Claims for Conventional Foods and Dietary Supplements." *US Food and Drug Administration*, 7 Mar. 2022, fda.gov. Accessed 6 July 2024.

3. Holly Riddle. "The Untold Truth of Naked Juice." *Mashed*, 7 Oct. 2021, mashed.com. Accessed 6 July 2024.

4. Nina Lakhani et al. "The Illusion of Choice: Five Stats That Expose America's Food Monopoly Crisis." *Guardian*, 18 July 2021, theguardian.com. Accessed 6 July 2024.

5. Julia Agostino. "Research Suggests 73% of Food in the US Is Ultra-Processed." *Food Tank*, 30 Nov. 2022, foodtank.com. Accessed 18 Apr. 2024.

6. Carol Ryan. "Are Ultra-Processed Foods Fattening? They Are for Company Profits." *Wall Street Journal*, 3 Feb. 2024, wsj.com. Accessed 18 Apr. 2024.

7. Michael Moss. *Hooked*. Random House, 2021. XXV.

8. Jennifer L. Harris et al. "Rudd Report." *UConn Rudd Center*, Nov. 2022, uconruddcenter.org. Accessed 6 July 2024.

9. "Targeted Marketing 2022 Executive Summary." *UConn Rudd Center*, Nov. 2022, uconnruddcenter.org. Accessed 10 May 2024.

10. Owen Walsh. "Food Deserts: What They Are and What Causes Them." *Humane League*, 22 Feb. 2022, thehumaneleague.org. Accessed 6 July 2024.

11. Nicole Rogers. "What Is a Food Hub?" *Sustainable America*, 26 Aug. 2013, sustainableamerica.org. Accessed 18 Apr. 2024.

CHAPTER 7. MARKETING TO CHILDREN

1. Jeff Cronin. "No Decline in Junk-Food Advertising on Children's Television." *Center for Science in the Public Interest*, 16 Feb. 2022, cspinet.org. Accessed 6 July 2024.

2. "Disney Says No to Junk-Food Ads on Kids' Shows." *CNBC*, 5 June 2012, cnbc.com. Accessed 18 Apr. 2024.

3. Amaal Alruwaily et al. "Child Social Media Influencers and Unhealthy Product Placement." *Pediatrics*, vol. 146, no. 5, 26 Oct. 2020.

4. Taren Swindle et al. "Pester Power." *Journal of Nutrition Education and Behavior*, vol. 52, no. 8, Aug. 2020. 801.

5. Kristin Messina. "Rudd Center: New Study Finds Fast-Food Companies Spending More on Advertising, Disproportionately Targeting Black and Latino Youth." *UConn Today*, 17 June 2021, today.uconn.edu. Accessed 6 July 2024.

6. "Unhealthy and Unregulated: Food Advertising and Marketing to Children." *American Heart Association*, 9 Apr. 2019, heart.org. Accessed 6 July 2024.

7. Roni Neff. *Introduction to the US Food System*. Jossey-Bass & Pfeiffer, 2014. 250.

8. "Guidance for Food Advertising Self-Regulation." *National Advertising Review Council*, 2004, corpora.tika.apache.org. Accessed 6 July 2024.

9. Jonathan Wald. "US Judge Dismisses Obesity Suit vs. McDonald's." *CNN Money*, 7 Feb. 2003, money.cnn.com. Accessed 18 Apr. 2024.

10. Missy Green. "Loopholes Still Permit US Brands to Advertise Unhealthy F&B to Children." *Nutrition Insight*, 5 Apr. 2022, nutritioninsight.com. Accessed 18 Apr. 2024.

11. "Shrek Boosts Vidalia Onion Sales." *ABC News*, 29 June 2010, abcnews.go.com. Accessed 12 May 2024.

12. "Nickelodeon and Birds Eye Announce Some of the Best Recipes They Received from Children." *NickALive!*, 8 Nov. 2012, nickalive.net. Accessed 18 Apr. 2024.

CHAPTER 8. MARKETING A BETTER FUTURE

1. "Modern Food Emissions." *Nature Climate Change*, vol. 13, no. 3, 1 Mar. 2023. 202–205.

2. "Irrigation & Water Use." *US Department of Agriculture*, 8 Sept. 2023, ers.usda.gov. Accessed 12 May 2024.

3. "Statistics and Facts." *Environmental Protection Agency*, 23 Jan. 2017, epa.gov. Accessed 12 May 2024.

4. Dee-Ann Durbin and David McHugh. "Meat from Plants." *Associated Press News*, 16 Nov. 2023, projects.apnews.com. Accessed 12 May 2024.

5. "Retail Sales Data: Plant-Based Meat, Eggs, Dairy." *Good Food Institute*, 2021, gfi.org. Accessed 12 May 2024.

6. Barbara Grady. "5 Years In, How Does General Mills' Regenerative Agriculture Commitment Measure Up?" *Green Biz*, 18 Jan. 2024, greenbiz.com. Accessed 12 May 2024.

7. Whitney Bauck. "New York Is Suing the World's Biggest Meat Company. It Might Be a Tipping Point for Greenwashing." *Guardian*, 5 Apr. 2024, theguardian.com. Accessed 12 May 2024.

8. "The Economic Cost of Food Monopolies: The Grocery Cartels." *Food and Water Watch*, Nov. 2021, foodandwaterwatch.org. Accessed 10 May 2024.

9. Eric Schlosser. "Do We Really Want a Food Cartel?" *Atlantic*, 9 Apr. 2024, theatlantic.com. Accessed 18 Apr. 2024.

10. Timothy Inklebarger. "Walmart, Kroger, Costco Make Top Three Grocery Retailers List." *Supermarket News*, 6 Mar. 2024, supermarketnews.com. Accessed 13 May 2024.

11. Marion Nestle. *Unsavory Truth: How Food Companies Skew the Science of What We Eat*. Basic Books, 2018. 231.

INDEX

KURT WALDENDORF

Kurt Waldendorf is the author of more than a dozen books for children. When he's not writing or editing, he enjoys indoor rock climbing and running along the shore of Lake Michigan with his dog. He lives in Chicago.